Buddha
in My Pocket

Buddha
in My Pocket

Christina Rodenbeck

RYLAND
PETERS
& SMALL
LONDON NEW YORK

Designer Saskia Janssen
Editor Miriam Hyslop
Picture Researcher Emily Westlake
Production Controller Deborah Wehner
Art Director Gabriella Le Grazie
Publishing Director Alison Starling

First published in the
United States in 2004
by Ryland Peters & Small, Inc.
519 Broadway
5th Floor
New York NY 10012
www.rylandpeters.com

10 9 8 7 6 5 4 3 2 1

Introduction, selection, commentaries text,
and design © Ryland Peters & Small 2004
For photography copyright see page 64.

ISBN 1 84172 731 8

Printed in China

Contents

Introduction

THE BUDDHA CAN ONLY TELL YOU THE WAY:
IT IS FOR YOU TO MAKE THE EFFORT YOURSELF.

Siddhartha Gautama was born about two and a half thousand years ago into a wealthy family in India. But he found he was more interested in solving the mysteries of life—such as why there is suffering—than living a life of luxury. His spiritual searching took him all over the continent until one day he had a flash of insight. Soon he had gathered disciples around him. They called him Buddha—"the Awakened One." Today, his followers number in their millions, his icon is one of the most widely recognized images in the world, and his teachings still speak to believers and non-believers alike. The wisdom of the Buddha crosses cultural and religious boundaries, speaking to us on a higher level than mere dogma. The words of the Buddha, some of which are given here, encourage us to ask questions and to think deeply. Buddhist philosophy asks us to look at the world afresh.

Essential Buddhism

Buddha's flash of insight that day was to understand Right Knowledge. This led him to formulate the eightfold path, which is the core of Buddhist belief. The goal of Buddhists is to reach a state of peace—nirvana—by following this "middle way" or path of selflessness.

The Noble Eightfold Path

- RIGHT KNOWLEDGE: *to see life as it really is. There are two parts to Buddha's worldview. First, according to the Buddha, life is continuously changing—nothing is fixed; furthermore, what we see and experience on the material level is an illusion anyway. Reality is hidden behind a kind of veil, which we must learn to tear away or see through. Secondly, one must follow the four noble truths: life is full of suffering, suffering is caused by our desire and ignorance, the end of suffering is the aim of life, the way to end suffering is to follow the eightfold path.*

- RIGHT MINDEDNESS: *to feel loving kindness towards all beings.*
- RIGHT SPEECH: *to speak kindly and truthfully at all times.*
- RIGHT ACTION: *to act with skill and sympathy and avoid needless action or violence.*
- RIGHT LIVELIHOOD: *to have a way of making a living that does not cause oneself or others to behave immorally.*
- RIGHT ENDEAVOUR: *to attempt to perfect oneself by getting rid of bad habits and cultivating good ones.*
- RIGHT MINDFULNESS: *to cultivate self-awareness and compassion which results in self-reliance and equanimity.*
- RIGHT CONCENTRATION: *to practice the concentration that achieves a kind of intellectual intuition. Many Buddhist sayings aim to bring this about by forcing you to think about a situation in a new way.*

Buddhism Today

Different interpretations of the eightfold way have led to Buddhism evolving into divergent sects. These strands of belief can appear quite unlike one another—Tibetan Buddhism with its rich, complex pantheon could almost seem the opposite of austere Japanese Zen. But the Buddha's own words live on and have an especial appeal today—not because they hark back to some golden age but because they are relevant to the times in which we find ourselves now. Buddhism is not about dogma; it is about attitude. The Buddhist way is about living life truthfully, kindly, and in the moment. But the Buddha himself said that "One should not found or follow any organized system of philosophy either by word or deed." Think about that.

The Three Main Schools of Buddhism

There's a myriad of sects but all of them fall into one of these schools:

- THERAVADA *(Hinayana; the Lesser Vehicle) in Burma, Thailand, Vietnam, Sri Lanka.*
- MAHAYANA *(the Greater Vehicle) in Tibet, Mongolia, China, Korea, Japan.*
- VAJRAYANA *(the Diamond Vehicle/Esoteric or Tantric Buddhism) mainly in Tibet.*

Knowledge

We are the result of
what we have thought.

The person who never
thinks: "This is mine,
that is hers,"
does not see herself
as at a disadvantage.

The fool believes an
evil deed is as delicious
as nectar—as long as
it does not bear fruit.
But when it ripens,
the taste will be bitter.

15

When a person, seeing you
practice goodness, comes
and insults you,
endure it patiently.
Do not feel angry with him,
for he insults himself.

When partisans start to
argue, each convinced
that his or her side is right,
tell them straight
that you are not interested.

People who are taken in
by appearances and go
around airing their views
are a constant source of
irritation in this world.

Thoughtfulness is a
valuable treasure.

If you come across a
true friend, a noble
and wise companion,
then thoughtful
and fearless, prosper
with your dear comrade.
If you do not meet
such a person, roam alone
like an exiled king.

"What is the most valuable thing in the world?"
the student asked the master.
"The head of a dead cat."
"What?" exclaimed the student. "Why?"
"Because no one," the master replied,
"can name its price."

ZEN KOAN

They are never happy
who praise those worthy
of blame or blame
those worthy of praise.

A person who is led by
his senses will become
the slave of an organization.

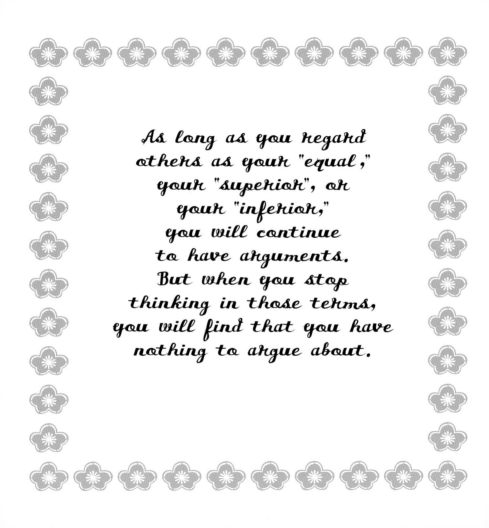

As long as you regard others as your "equal," your "superior", or your "inferior," you will continue to have arguments. But when you stop thinking in those terms, you will find that you have nothing to argue about.

It is hopeless to look
for guidance to a person
with rigid ideas.

People hold on to their worldly possessions and selfish passions so blindly that they end up sacrificing their whole lives to them. They are like a child who tries to eat a little honey from the blade of a knife. The amount is too small to satisfy his hunger, and the knife is sharp enough to cut his tongue.

A fool who thinks that
he is a fool is, for
that reason, wise.
The fool who thinks
that he is wise is
called a fool indeed.

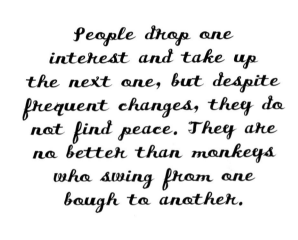

People drop one
interest and take up
the next one, but despite
frequent changes, they do
not find peace. They are
no better than monkeys
who swing from one
bough to another.

31

Eight Lucky Buddhist Symbols

Parasol
Pair of fishes
Treasure vase
Lotus
Conch shell
Endless knot
Victory banner
Golden wheel

*A single
quietening word
is better than
a long speech.*

33

Compassion

The sooner the wish
to injure disappears,
the sooner suffering
will stop.

As a mother loves
her child one should
cherish all living beings.
Radiating loving-kindness
over the entire world—
upwards to the sky,
down to the depths, all
around—one's heart
grows great, wide, deep,
boundless, free from
hatred, and ill-will.

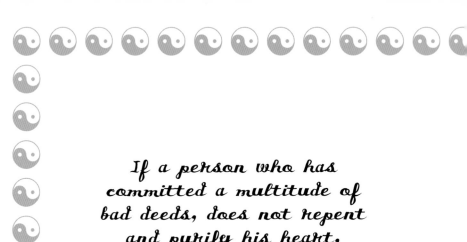

If a person who has committed a multitude of bad deeds, does not repent and purify his heart, retribution will come as sure as the stream running into the ocean grows ever deeper and wider. But if a person who has committed

the same bad deeds, comes
to recognize his mistakes,
reforms and practices
goodness, the force of
retribution will gradually
exhaust itself in the same
way that a disease
gradually loses its grip as
the patient sweats.

Calm mind;
Calm speech;
Calm movement;
Through right knowledge,
the sage is completely free:
Perfectly peaceful,
perfectly balanced.

Overcome anger with love,
ill will by good will;
overcome the greedy
with generosity, and
the liar with truth.

Have nothing; want nothing.

The family is a place where minds
come into contact with one
another. If these minds love one
another, the home will be as
beautiful as a flower garden.

Hatreds never defeat
hatreds in this world.
Love alone ends hatred.

The sweetness of truth
surpasses all sweetness.

The Four Immeasurables

Following these four principles is the center of Buddhist practice.

BENEVOLENCE: *the desire to establish all sentient beings in a state of happiness and to establish them in the cause of happiness.*
COMPASSION: *the desire to free them from suffering and to remove the cause of their suffering.*
SYMPATHY: *delight in the happiness of others.*
EQUANIMITY: *the attitude that not one sentient being is more or less important than another. No attachment is felt towards one or aversion towards another.*

Wisdom

Don't dwell on other people's faults—things that they have done or left undone.

Why does the enlightened person
not stand on his feet
and speak for himself?

ZEN KOAN

Nirvana is awakening
from a day dream
or nightmare.

On the long journey
of human life, faith is the
best of companions; it is
the best refreshment and it
is the greatest possession.

Faith gives the wisdom to recognize the transience of life, and grace not to be surprised or grieved at whatever comes to pass or even at death itself.

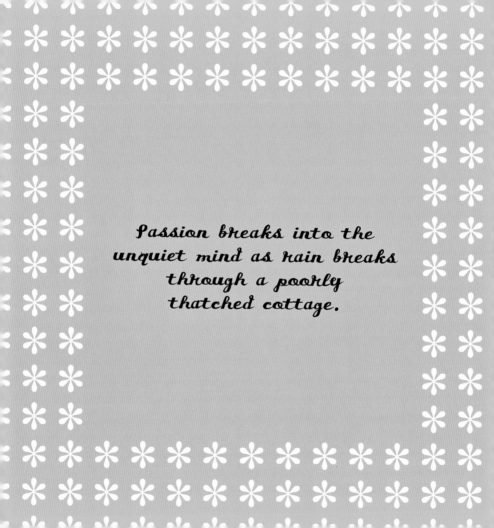

Passion breaks into the
unquiet mind as rain breaks
through a poorly
thatched cottage.

57

Awake among the oblivious, wide awake among the sleeping. The wise one advances like a thorough bred leaving a nag behind.

Like a bee taking honey
from a blossom,
leaving its color and
scent intact,
so should a sage wander
in the village.

Before enlightenment,
chop wood and carry water.
After enlightenment,
chop wood and carry water.

ANON

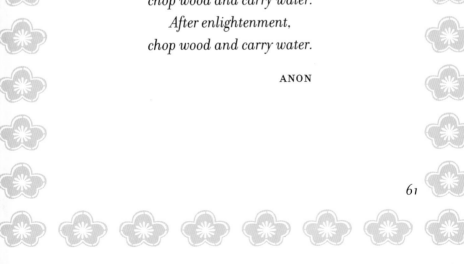

Death parts a person from everything he labeled "mine." Wise is the person who owns nothing.

Let the past go
Let the future go
Let the present go
Release your mind
from everything.

Picture credits

Jacket & 3 © Dominic Arizona Bonuccelli/azfoto.com; 11 © Gabriella Le Grazie; 13 © Chris Mellor/Lonely Planet Images; 16 © Felicity Volk/Lonely Planet Images; 21 © Adrian Baker/International Photobank; 24 © Anders Blomqvist/Lonely Planet Images; 29 © Gabriella Le Grazie; 32 © Martin Llado/Lonely Planet Images; 34 © Nicholas Reuss/Lonely Planet Images; 41 © Saskia Janssen; 44 © World Religions Photo Library /Claire Stout; 49 © Dominic Arizona Bonuccelli/azfoto.com; 52 © Steve Lovegrove/Picture Tasmania; 57 © Steve MacAulay /www.stevemacaulayphotography.com; 60 Catherine Gratwicke; 63 © UPPA/Bandphoto

Bibliography

Allen, G F (trans); **Buddha's Words of Wisdom**; George Allen and Unwin Ltd, 1959
Percheron, Maurice; **Buddha and Buddhism**; Longmans, 1957
Reps, Paul; **Zen Flesh, Zen Bones**; Charles E. Tuttle Co, 1959
Woodward, F L (trans); **Some Sayings of the Buddha**; The Buddhist Society London. 1973
The Teaching of Buddha; Bukkyo Dendo Kyokai, 1996